Capstone Short Biographies

Native American Scientists

Fred Begay, Wilfred F. Denetclaw Jr., Frank C. Dukepoo, Clifton Poodry, Jerrel Yakel

by Jetty St. John

CAPSTONE PRESS

MANKATO

C A P S T O N E P R E S S
818 North Willow Street • Mankato, MN 56001

Printed in the United States of America.

Library of Congress Cataloging-in-Publication Data
St. John, Jetty.
    Native American scientists/by Jetty St. John
    p. cm.
    Includes bibliographical references and index.
    Summary: Presents five brief biographies of Native Americans who have pursued careers in various scientific fields: Jerrel Yakel, Clifton Poodry, Frank C. Dukepoo, Wilfred F. Denetclaw Jr., and Fred Begay.
    ISBN 1-56065-359-0
    1. Scientists--United States--Biography--Juvenile literature. [1. Scientists. 2. Indians of North America--Biography.]
    Q141.K249 1996
    509.2'273--dc20

                                                                95-50305
                                                                   CIP
                                                                    AC

Photo credits
Jean S. Buldain: 4, 18
Felix Farrar: 6, 14
Los Alamos National Laboratory: cover and 22
Danny Lehman: 25, 26
James P. Rowan: 42
National Institute of Environmental Health Sciences/Steve McCaw: 34
University of Minnesota/Center for Magnetic Resonance Research: 36, 37

Table of Contents

Words in **boldface** type in the text are defined
in the Glossary in the back of this book.

Chapter 1

What Is a Scientist?

Scientists are curious about the world. They ask many questions. They talk to other people with the same questions. All of them are looking for answers.

When scientists cannot find an answer, they make a guess. The guess is called a hypothesis. Scientists do experiments to test the hypothesis.

If the experiment works, the scientist tells other people about it. Often they write articles about the experiment for science magazines.

Monument Valley, in northern Arizona and southern Utah, is located on the Navajo Indian reservation.

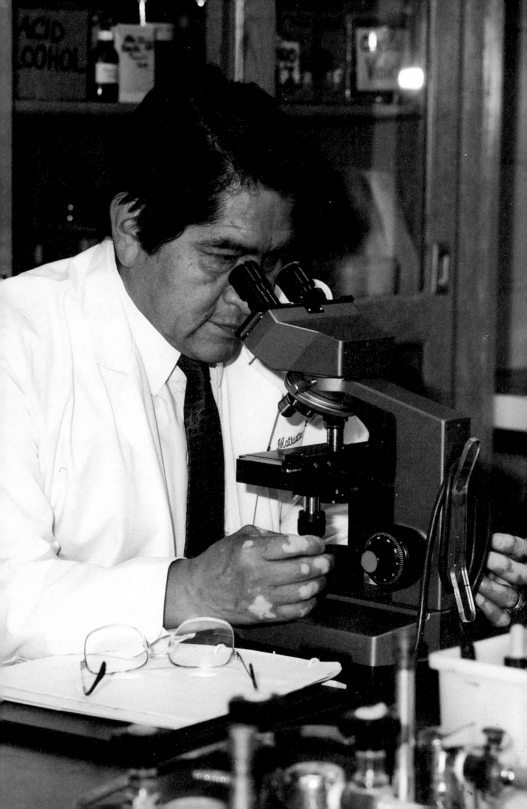

Other scientists repeat the original experiment. If everyone gets the same results, the hypothesis is accepted as a fact.

At Work

Scientists study birds, animals, and plants. They study the weather, stars, rock formations, heat, and light. They study anything in the natural world. Scientists often work in teams.

They learn even when experiments go wrong. Scientists never give up searching for answers.

Native American Scientists

This book will introduce you to five Native American scientists. They are from several different Indian tribes. They decided to become scientists for different reasons. They are experts in different fields. They all enjoy being scientists and helping others through their work.

Frank C. Dukepoo is a geneticist. He was the first Hopi to get a doctorate in science.

Chapter 2

Wilfred F. Denetclaw Jr.

Wilfred F. Denetclaw Jr. was born in 1959. He is a Navajo who grew up in Shiprock, New Mexico. The small town is part of the Navajo Nation, an Indian reservation in the Four Corners area. Four states meet here. They are Arizona, Colorado, New Mexico, and Utah.

When he was young, Denetclaw helped care for cattle and sheep on his family's farm near Shiprock. Some of his lambs and calves were born strong and healthy. Others were weak and sick. Some died of mysterious illnesses. This early work with animals led to his interest in diseases that affect humans.

Wilfred F. Denetclaw Jr. is a zoologist. He works at the University of California in San Francisco.

Denetclaw studied biology at Fort Lewis College in Colorado. There were few other Indians studying science. This made him feel lonely.

He also faced a serious problem. He was asked to **dissect** a cat in anatomy class. Anatomy is the study of the parts that make up animals and plants. But Navajo are forbidden to disturb dead animals because this would disturb their spirits.

Denetclaw talked to a **medicine man** before deciding he had to dissect the cat. He hoped the Great Spirit would understand. As a scientist, he needed to know about animals' bodies.

Denetclaw went on to get a bachelor of science degree. He then got a **doctorate** in zoology at the University of California in Berkeley.

Advice from a Medicine Man

One day, Denetclaw went home to Shiprock to see a Navajo medicine man. He said he felt alone. Most of his people did not understand what he did in the lab. The medicine man told Denetclaw he was like a modern scout. In the old days, scouts

Wilfred Denetclaw Jr., who grew up in New Mexico, now lives in California.

explored new land. They searched for good places to take the tribe.

The medicine man said Denetclaw was working in an area where few Indians worked. This area was science. The medicine man said it might be a great place to take the rest of the tribe.

Denetclaw studies diseases that have no cure. Recently, a young Navajo man in the Four Corners area was taken to a hospital. Everyone thought he had the flu. But within a few hours, his lungs filled with fluid, and he died.

Other young people in the area died, too. They died within days of feeling sick. Denetclaw and other scientists worked furiously to find out why the people were dying.

Many scientists thought they found the answer. They said the cause of the deaths was a **virus** carried by wild deer mice.

The scientists said the **infected** mice passed the virus to the soil through their droppings. When the wind blew, the soil mixed with the air. They thought people breathed in the virus that way.

Denetclaw, however, is not so sure. People from different parts of the country have died of the disease. The virus was not found in their bodies.

He thinks many questions need to be answered. A cure cannot be found until scientists know for sure what causes the illness.

Disease Affects Boys

Denetclaw is studying another disease called Duchenne muscular dystrophy. One out of 4,000 boys is born with the disease. It causes a young boy's muscles to weaken and break down. Almost no girls get the disease.

Wilfred Denetclaw Jr. encourages teens to take math and science classes.

Scientists have found a **gene** that causes the disease. Denetclaw hopes a cure can be found now.

Denetclaw works at the University of California in San Francisco. He studies chicken **embryos.** He is learning more about the way muscles develop.

He is a modern scout. He encourages teens to take math and science classes. He hopes there will be many more Indian scientists. They can help find cures for diseases that affect people everywhere.

Chapter 3

Frank C. Dukepoo

Frank C. Dukepoo was born in 1943. He was one of 13 children and grew up on the Hopi reservation in Arizona. He was originally named Pumatuhye Tsi Dukpuh. Pumatuhye means first crop. Tsi Dukpuh refers to the sack carried by Hopi snake dancers. They pray for rain to help the crops grow.

Pumatuhye Tsi Dukpuh went to a white school in third grade. There he was called Frank C. Dukepoo.

He was a skinny child. The class bully picked on him. They fought one day on the playground. Dukepoo was knocked to the ground. He was angry.

He knew his father would not approve of fistfights. Hopi means peaceful ones. He decided he would outsmart the bully in the classroom.

Frank C. Dukepoo teaches biology at Northern Arizona University in Flagstaff.

High school was easy for Dukepoo. After graduation, he was accepted at the University of Arizona. He had five scholarships. But he did not study at college. He just wanted to have a good time. He went to parties and ball games and played the saxophone.

Dukepoo flunked his first semester. His grades were mostly Ds and Fs. He lost his scholarships. He was broke. He asked the Great Spirit for help.

One of his biology professors was Charles Woolf. He liked Dukepoo. He saw that Dukepoo was excited about science.

From the Great Spirit, Dukepoo got courage. And he got advice from Woolf, who told him to earn the money he needed. Then he could start school again. Dukepoo found a job sweeping floors on campus. He improved his grades. Eventually, he got a bachelor's degree in biology. All through school, Dukepoo knew Woolf had confidence in him.

He got a **master's degree** and a doctorate in **zoology**. He had special training in **genetics.**

Frank C. Dukepoo went to grade school in Phoenix, Arizona.

Dukepoo proudly returned to his people. He was the first Hopi to get a doctorate in science.

Dukepoo is a geneticist. He studies the differences between people. He learns about genes and how they are responsible for the differences.

We all have genes. They are like special blueprints in our body. They determine every part of us. They decide the color of our eyes. They decide the thickness of our hair and whether it is curly or straight.

Monument Valley Navajo Tribal Park is in northern Arizona near the Utah border. (Photo next page)

Genes are passed from parents to their children. Half of the genes come from the mother and half come from the father.

Albinism

Dukepoo is interested in a genetic condition called albinism. People and animals with albinism are called albinos. They lack **pigment** in their skin, hair, and eyes.

One in every 10,000 people in the world has albinism. It occurs more often among Dukepoo's people. One of every 227 Hopi is born with albinism.

People with albinism have white hair. Their eyes look pink or blue. They have red pupils. Their eyes are sensitive to sunlight. They are likely to get skin cancer. Albinism occurs more often in blacks, Hispanics, and Indians than it does in whites.

The condition is passed on through families. Dukepoo visits Hopi and Navajo families and takes blood samples from each family member. He studies them in his lab. He is looking for the

Frank C. Dukepoo visits Virgie Charlie, right. She and 10 of her brothers and sisters have albinism.

gene that causes albinism. When the gene is found, then a cure might be found for albinism.

Dukepoo teaches biology at Northern Arizona University. When he is not in his lab, he is on the Hopi reservation. He wants to give health and hope to his people.

Dukepoo is a teacher as well as a scientist. He started the Native American Honor Society. Students of all ages can join if they get straight As for one quarter. He believes that if he managed to turn bad grades into good grades, then others can, too.

Chapter 4

Fred Begay

Fred Begay was born in 1932. His father
and mother were from the Navajo and Ute
tribes. They called their son Clever Fox
because he was a skillful hunter. It was his job
to feed the four younger children in his family.
He shot deer and trapped rabbits near his home
in Towaoc, Colorado.

When he was nine years old, his mother told
him to follow the river for 15 miles. He would
reach a school for Indian children. They would
give him food and shelter.

The government school was run by whites.
Begay had only seen white people once before.
He was surprised that they lived in houses

**Fred Begay is a physicist at Los Alamos National
Laboratory in Los Alamos, New Mexico.**

instead of tents. They had so much food, they threw it away. He dug through the garbage for fruit and vegetables.

At his new school, Indian children were not allowed to speak the Navajo language. Fred Begay's name was changed to Fred Young. He did not see his family for two years. He was not allowed to attend Indian religious ceremonies.

After leaving school, Begay joined the U.S. Army. He flew on rescue missions during the Korean War (1950-1953). When he returned from the war, his tribe paid for him to go to the University of New Mexico.

Graduated with Honors

Begay studied many hours a day. He was excited about science. It answered his questions about nature. He also studied philosophy. It helped him understand white people.

Begay felt alone. His Navajo ways taught him not to stand out in a crowd. In his

Medicine man Atcitty Begay kneels beside physicist Fred Begay near Shiprock on the Navajo reservation.

language, the word "special" does not exist. Because he was quiet, people thought he was stupid or afraid. This made Begay angry. But he never gave up his studies.

He graduated with honors. He received a bachelor of science degree in physics and math in 1961. Then he received his master's degree. He followed it with a doctorate in physics in 1971.

Fred Begay displays a Navajo sand painting.

After college, Begay went to work at the Los Alamos National Laboratory in New Mexico. Los Alamos is where the first atom bomb was made in 1945. The atom bomb split atoms apart. Begay, though, is working to join atoms to produce heat.

He has designed experiments that were sent into space on rockets. Begay wants to learn more about the heat coming from the sun. He is trying to discover a way to produce affordable heat without harming the environment.

Teaching His People

Begay returns to his reservation in the Four Corners area often. He tells people about the work he does in the lab. Once he tried to explain how he measures the sun's heat with **laser beams.** The medicine men did not understand how Begay's work could help the Navajo.

Many Navajo live without heat or running water in their homes. For them, the sun is something they pray to. They look to the sun for protection and guidance.

Begay said he is copying the way the sun works. Then he might be able to bring heat and electricity to reservation homes.

Chapter 5

Clifton Poodry

Clifton Poodry is a member of the Seneca tribe. He was born in 1943 and grew up on the Tonawanda Seneca Reservation in western New York.

He went to the University of Buffalo in New York. He was planning to become a high-school science teacher and football coach.

He was not motivated to study hard until he learned about genetics. Suddenly, he became fascinated by the way creatures develop from a single cell. He earned a master's degree in genetics.

He received his doctorate in biology from Case Western Reserve University in 1971. For 22 years, he was a professor of biology at the University of California in Santa Cruz.

Clifton Poodry works at the National Institutes of Health.

Scottie Henderson studies seals in South America. She conducted research with Clifton Poodry in college.

The Fruit Fly

On Poodry's license plate it says FRU FLY. It is short for fruit fly. Scientists are excited about this little insect. By studying the fruit fly, scientists are learning how living creatures develop from a single cell into a complex organism made of millions of cells.

The instructions coded in the fruit fly's genes tell some cells to become eyes and others to form the head or body. No one knows exactly how this happens. The process is controlled by the special genetic code inside the cells.

Genetics

Half of the genetic code in any living thing comes from its mother. The other half comes from its father. Genetic instructions are found in each cell. They are in units called **chromosomes.**

Humans have 46 chromosomes. Fruit flies have only four. Fruit fly chromosomes are large. They are easy to study.

Scientists like Poodry want to understand genetic patterns. They want to know where to find each gene. They hope to understand what each gene does.

Poodry hopes to apply what he learns from fruit flies to human genes. Scientists all over the world are working together to map human genes. They hope to treat genetic conditions that cause illness and death.

Clifton Poodry, left, meets with students Rudy Gamboa, center, and Scottie Henderson at a meeting of the American Indian Society of Engineering and Science.

Teacher

Today, Poodry works at the National Institutes of Health in Maryland. He is the director of Minority Opportunities in Research.

He uses his skills as a scientist and as a teacher to help students get the education they need. In the past, girls and minorities have not been encouraged to develop technical and scientific skills. Poodry wants to help them get equal opportunities.

He is especially interested in helping teachers of Native American children learn more about science. Then they can pass the information on to their students. Poodry believes that by working hard as a scientist and by sharing his knowledge, his work will have an impact for many years.

Scottie Henderson

One of Poodry's students was Scottie Henderson, a Navajo from New Mexico. Henderson did research with Poodry at the University of California at Santa Cruz. He helped her learn about marine animals. He taught her about genetic differences.

Henderson received her bachelor of arts degree in marine biology and is working toward her doctorate. She spends most of the year at the Friday Harbor Marine Lab on San Juan Island, north of Seattle. The island and lab were featured in the movie *Free Willy 2*. During the winter, she is at the University of Washington in Seattle.

With other scientists, Henderson studies elephant seals off the shores of Patagonia in Argentina.

Chapter 6

Jerrel Yakel

Jerrel Yakel was born in 1959. He grew up in Ventura County, California. His father, who is white, is a retired police officer. His mother is a Luiseno Indian and a member of the La Jolla tribe. Yakel enjoyed being part of two cultures.

He went to **powwows** with his mother and grandparents. There, he took part in traditional dancing, feasts, and ceremonies. He also helped his grandparents sell fry bread at the county fair. Fry bread is an Indian specialty. It is like a doughnut but not as sweet.

Yakel's eighth grade science teacher asked him to collect and study 50 different kinds of insects. This got Yakel interested in science.

Jerrel Yakel is a neuroscientist at the National Institute of Environmental Health Sciences in North Carolina.

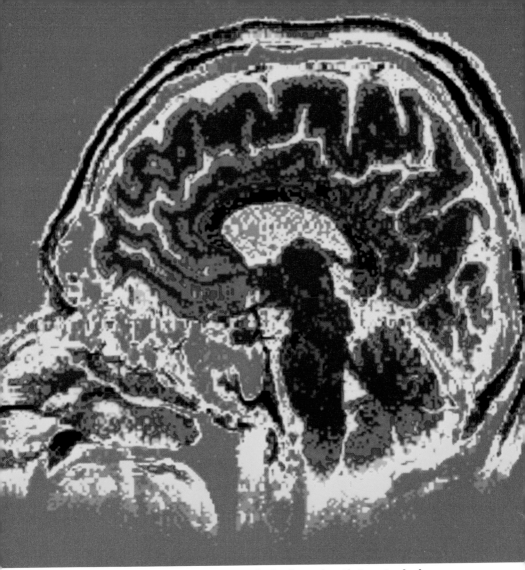

Colorful images of the brain help scientists study how the brain works.

Yakel earned a doctorate in neurobiology from the University of California at Los Angeles. He studies the way the brain works. If he learns how it works, he may be able to find cures for brain diseases.

Today, Jerrel Yakel is a top neuroscientist. He works at the National Institute of Environmental Health Sciences in North Carolina.

Jerrel Yakel and other scientists believe if they learn how the brain works they can find cures for brain diseases.

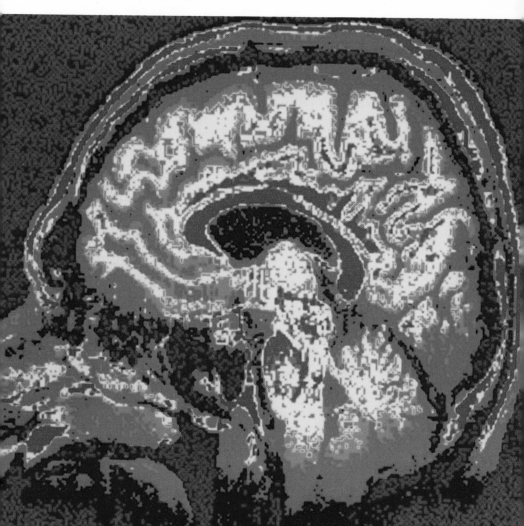

Messages in the Brain

Yakel studies the way messages travel in the brain. He and other scientist have learned that messages start as electric impulses and travel through nerves.

Electrical messages get changed to chemical messages when they reach the end of a nerve. Between the nerves are spaces called synapses. Yakel and other scientists know that most communication takes place in these spaces.

Understanding Diseases

The brain controls our muscles. It is the center for emotions, memories, and thoughts. It makes up our personalities. The brain works better if it has good connections.

Yakel and other scientists hope to understand such diseases as depression, schizophrenia, epilepsy, and Alzheimer's.

Some of these diseases are caused by genes. Others are caused by chemical imbalances.

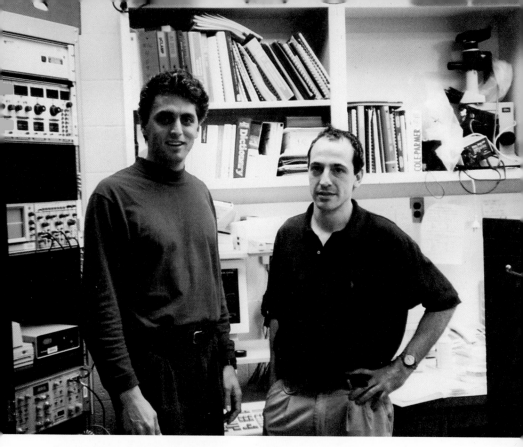

Jerrel Yakel, left, worked with Belgian scientist Patrick Gilon in the laboratory.

Some are affected by aging. Cures for these diseases can be found only by understanding how the brain works.

Jerrel Yakel is married to Melody Butterfield. He graduated from Oregon State University in 1981.

Discoveries and Hopes

Sometimes people suffer brain injuries. Other people may need surgery to remove diseased parts of the brain.

Yakel and other scientists have found that one part of the brain will sometimes take over the work of missing or damaged parts. They think new nerve endings might grow with the help of special medicines.

Spreading the Message

Because of his work on the brain, Yakel travels all over the world. He meets scientists from many different countries and learns new ideas.

Yakel thinks people should keep learning as much as they can. He thinks it is important to have an open mind.

Glossary

cell—small complex unit that makes up all living things

chromosome—structure in a cell containing genetic codes that control growth, development, and function of all cells

dissect—to cut something apart piece by piece in order to study it

doctorate—the highest degree awarded by a college or university

embryo—an animal in an early form of development in an egg or uterus

gene—physical and behavioral information passed from parents to their children

genetics—a branch of biology that deals with heredity and differences in similar or related animals and plants

infect—transmit a disease to an animal or plant

Scientists study the natural world from the dry deserts of the American southwest to the lush islands of Hawaii.

laser beam—narrow, intense beam of light used in surgery, cutting metal, communications, and measuring devices
master's degree—a college or university degree awarded after graduate study
medicine man—Native American who presides at ceremonies and is said to cure diseases and control spirits
pigment—substance that adds color to a cell
powwow—Native American gathering, conference, or ceremony
virus—tiny particle that invades cells and causes disease
zoology—scientific study of animals

To Learn More

Aronson, Billy. *They Came From DNA*. New York: Scientific American Books for Young Readers, 1993.

Grace, Eric S. *Seals*. Boston: Little, Brown, 1991.

Metos, Thomas H. *The Human Mind: How We Think and Learn*. New York: Franklin Watts, 1990.

Waldman, Carl. *Encyclopedia of Native American Tribes*. New York: Facts on File, 1988.

Wolfson, Evelyn. *From Abenaki to Zuni: A Dictionary of Native American Tribes*. New York: Walker, 1988.

Wu, Norbert. *Life in the Oceans*. Boston: Little, Brown, 1991.

Useful Addresses

Albinism World Alliance
1500 Locust Street, Suite 2405
Philadelphia, PA 19102-4318

Canadian Genetic Diseases Network
2125 East Mall, Room 348
Vancouver, BC V6T 1Z4
Canada

Marine Biomedical Institute
2101 Constitution Avenue
Washington, DC 20418

National Native American Honor Society
P.O. Box 5640
Northern Arizona University
Flagstaff, AZ 86011-5640

Society for the Advancement of Chicanos and Native Americans in Science
University of California
Sinsheimer Labs
Santa Cruz, CA 95064

Society for Canadian Women in Science and Technology
515 Hastings Street, Suite 80
Calgary, AB T3B 0M6
Canada

United National Indian Tribal Youth
P.O. Box 25042
4010 Lincoln Boulevard, Suite 202
Oklahoma City, OK 73125

Index